JEFF OAKS

Little What

LILY POETRY REVIEW BOOKS

Published by Lily Poetry Review Books
223 Winter Street
Whitman, MA 02382

https://lilypoetryreview.blog/

ISBN:978-1-7337683-3-7

Cover Design: Martha McCollough
Cover Art: Morning Interior, Jeff Oaks

To make others believe, we must believe ourselves.

—Bachelard

ACKNOWLEDGEMENTS:

Thanks to the editors where these poems first appeared:

About Place: "Honey"
Assaracus: "Parsnips," "The Violets"
Barrow Street: "Midlife"
Bloom: "Mistakes with Strangers," "Little What"
Field: "Having Read Tranströmer All Night," "For the Small Hairs
of My Nose"
hanging loose: "Shift"
HeART: "The Morning Birds"
la fovea: "The Equipage"
Nashville Review: "Salt"
North American Review: "The Dream of the Grandfathers"
Ocean State Review: "The Song"
Poemeleon: "Saint Wrench"
Portable BOOG Reader: "The Moon"
Ploughshares: "Emptying the Octopus"
Superstition Review: "Sand," "Sunflower"
Tinderbox Poetry Review: "Queer: some instructions"
Zocalo Public Square: "The Drunk," "The Nests in Winter," "Begin"

"Saint Wrench" was chosen for *Best New Poets 2012*, edited
by Matthew Dickman, Meridian Press.

Some of these poems appeared in two limited edition chapbooks,
Shift (2010) and *Mistakes with Strangers* (2014), both from Seven Kitchens Press.
Thanks to Ron Mohring for his support and beautiful work.

Special thanks to the Pennsylvania Council on the Arts for three
literature fellowships which helped make some space and time to work
on this manuscript.

I am grateful to so many people but especially to Geeta Kothari, Jenny Johnson,
Jan Freeman, Liz Ahl, Deb Bogen, Noah Stetzer, Ron Mohring, Brandon Som,
and Stacey Waite for for friendship, for support, and for reading parts or all of
this book. Thanks as well to Eileen Cleary and Martha McCollough for their
beautiful work.

1

2

3

4

Little What

1

Begin

Mystery who wanders the basement.
Mystery who kicks at the screen.
Mystery whose cowbells mean something is close
to appearing, to appearance.

Earth—Silence—open, don't keep shutting
or turning mysterious (refuse to be
Rome, Jerusalem, Babylon, old stones),
struggle forward toward me.

There is someone here, waiting, not angry.
Not even lonely. Similarly restless. Maybe
not even me either—watching the windows.
Tickle the wind chimes, wander the lawn.

Perhaps turn near the patio where someone—
not even me exactly—has left a full mug
of tea, sweet, milky, not even steaming
anymore.   No one knows why.   Not here at least.

The phone didn't ring. I wasn't hungry.
Nothing like the dog howling at the mailman.
No neighbor needing help. I just stood up—
but not me necessarily—and went back to my life

to find it missing—or maybe it was me then.
Mystery, knock. The laundry can go on
being uninhabited. There is vodka in the freezer
so cold it might make a voice tangible, easier.

The Old War

You'd bring a stick with a rag tied to it
into the apple branches and light it,
touch the complicated gauzes
of the tent caterpillars until they smoked
like an old harem in the hands of a new king,
and charred, small bodies began falling.
The flame had a strange color, like a texture,
the smoke catching and escaping the branches.
You had to be patient, deliberate, careful
not to burn the leaves left, the little fruit, only
touch the furious heat to the beddings
and the curtains, the tablecloths and the rugs,
all the spun netting. None of the libraries
could remain after, not one chamber, not
even the furthermost penthouse where
some years an apple might remain out
of anyone's reach, halfway to Mars.
Anything suffering we smashed underfoot,
a small kind of pleasure that pressure. Veil
after veil lifting, becoming ash, and later
at the carnival, you could taste it
in the cotton candy, the fireworks'
smoke drifting over the fields where space
was made for celebration, cakes, pies
for a price; the firemen ready for a falling spark
to surprise them—hoping maybe;
the old men still looking for Sputnik.

Parsnips

Roasted with salt and pepper. The pale kings
under the mountains. When did I start
chewing at the roots of things?
A young boy naked in moonlight
while my best friend asked me
questions. Both of us thin and white
as these bodies whose skin I flay,
whose sweet trunks I whittle
into slivers, cut into cubes.
When he moved close one night,
I didn't refuse what he wanted
to do. It's a wonder I kept
breathing. I thought
the heat he made rise in me
was blood and said
Stop, that's enough.
Later, at home
I took myself all
the way to what was
almost like
weeping in secret
it was so beautiful.

Sunflower

We don't have a good name for what
weakens the shell, cracks it open, makes us
step out into the light. First bees with
their powdered legs then small sparrows who
rain down seed-slivers over the sidewalk.
Why stand out here staring at the great flower
grown in a pot I nearly threw away? It
has a kind of stature for all its luck I
might say I lack. Although I am here
watching small birds remove each seed
with the cunning of jewelers. With all
the courage to continue. Without a name
for any of the things they don't have.

The Drunk

The wind is sharpening its knives
on my father come in the dark
toward home, half wreckage,
half-bear in Christ's cold garden.
His tongue is quit, tied,
flat: the journey shakes
in his steering. Father, father,
it is too far to the river.
Whatever you are
I didn't know. I couldn't.

The Moon

Who is it who has compassion for the soldier
who comes back from the war missing
the great horses? Who kisses the parts
turned phantom? Decides not to cry into dinner?
Who makes light of the right losses? Who doesn't need
to be clever? Let me kiss the face that survived the disaster,
that once smiled make smile. With whatever
swells and fades, sharpens and scars, dust and vacuum.
Whatever tangles in shadows like a search party coming.
Because something is always looking for a way out
of whatever it is we keep getting into. Or rather,
we keep seeing home in every mistaken turn.

Sand

Who isn't a boulder turned to dust? When
isn't there something in your eye, an ache
where there's been a blink? Who hasn't buried
a civilization or two out of laziness? Reverse
the hourglass and there's another hourglass.
How else can the salad or the oyster or clam
bite back? The wind's circular saws keen
against the claims of the ancient mountains
made out of collisions, burning under us.
Where there is no snow, there is still this
form of insistence which the worm learns
to avoid, the wasp to structure, the child
to shape all day into castles, his face
to the ocean heaving up discarded armors.

The Violets

Strangeness on simmer
in the corner
by the brickpile,

the violets
grow without an ounce
of self-pity,

a quiet flame
you can eat
if you're hungry,

in the shadow of the grill,
behind the snowshovel's
broken haft, the broom left

out to rot, flame in the crack
by the rake, in the lee
of the garbage cans,

a ruthless beauty—like
the ash of a burning school—eating
whatever dirt falls down.

The Morning Birds

Asks my student from Bosnia, *what*
is the name of those birds I hear
every morning singing in the dark?

I don't know, so I look it up.
The robin, the starling, the mockingbird.
Looking for mates, marking out space,

even in the darkness. Often from
the highest point it can find. Although
it might also be a fence full of sparrows

chattering like a waterfall among the diamond
shaped spaces of the chain link fences
everywhere around us or the wires running

from house to house with distractions.
One bird he says sounds *like the same*
as bullets whispering past your ear.

Another is saying Come Here, Come Here,
Come Here. That's a cardinal, I think.
The red bird? The blood-red bird?

At the Rescue

Each dog its separate nervousness. Some
press themselves against the bars to show
how good they'd be. Some sit in the corner,
watch to see who stops. Some jump up
for everyone. Some watch the latch.
All day visitors walk, stop,
rattle a clipboard for history, for reasons
to keep moving on. Most do.
It is useless to give away your heart
but hard not to. Otherwise the stark
plastic beds, the steel bowls of water,
the howl of a neighbor in the next stall.
Occasionally knees bend and a hand
comes close to the bars. And if the self
break out of the self, how? A bark,
a backing away, a long stare?
Hi buddy, hi pretty girl like a slow rain
while the cheap lights above whine,
a thin sheet falling everywhere. Some
have heads like bowling balls. Some have
ears like bats, clipped, docked, sharp.
It is a curse to be beautiful if you howl,
if you cannot be trusted not to tear
the insides out of couches, chairs, if
they will not bend to let you smell
their hands safe on the other side of the bars.
Muscular and fleet, one being walked
outside shits on the sidewalk explosively,
a mess no one can clean. Some
explode at cars or squirrels or
the vacuum's slender, cylindrical hose
and brushes. So far the mild fall
has mostly meant long walks in small parks where
in the fountain castaway bread stalls,
the ducks having flown off. Pigeons
stand around like bankers at a funeral.

Some dogs were found hungry and weak.
Some lived lives a leash long, summer and winter.
On the visitors' board, the tacked up testimonials:
Adopting X changed my life! Take
a chance on love! Can you open your heart?
Have you always told the truth?
Sometimes they tied his legs together.
This one was thrown away, out a window.
Fire, Lack, Stone, Metal. Every thought
you have had has happened outside
your studio door, somewhere in your city.
Every insidious thought. *Knows how to sit*
nevertheless. *Will give paw. Will need*
some socialization but walks well on leash.
Found in overcrowded conditions. Knows
how to dance, let her show you. Initially
shy but will flower with the right attention.
This far inland, after the infamous hurricane,
the orphaned one I walk can barely restrain
his urge to leave some mark on everything
he comes upon. He barely lifts his head
the whole time, desperate for any news.

2

Little What

In the darkness. What a sonnet. When muscle
grunts, gives, accepts, resists, sucks its breath,
even aches. But is not broken. What is going up.
Not a wrong way. What is going in. What is darkness
but unseen. Where are those nerves? There. What
a sonnet. Like a bed with a penis. Growing harder.
Like a hallway after grief. A curse and a whisper,
an awe, out of which the wolf arose. On your lap.
Nails clicking, down the finally dark purple
each man sits on quietly, secretly. A hyacinth. That
strange boy dead, transformed into petals. My
God. What a sonnet, what a little song of nails.
Slap it. Wolf it down. Slip it in, sing on. The mouth
shivers and opens to be a moan, that moon.

Mistakes with Strangers

I pulled down a man's pants in public once.
I had said *I love you* earlier and I had meant it.
Don't ask me why. Two men later I was him,
betrayed. I pulled off the next man's wings
in return and I found out he went on to own
and run a large company that manufactured
shoes so beautiful you had to buy them
but so heavy they were impossible to lift. Some people died.
Help me, Rhonda, Jesus is not coming for me.
I stopped returning his calls. His wounds
made a boring centerpiece for conversation.
He kept asking me to stick my finger in them
all the time. The next man stuck me
with a three-hundred-dollar sexline phone bill
and vanished. I liked his thick body that was like
an ice cream cone I could not lick away.
Later, I was told he was a professional
ice cream cone, whatever flavor you wanted,
at the corner of 6th and Wood downtown.
So I paid. One man I stuck with a three
year depression—well, *he* said— that required
a therapist, two women chiropractors, three new jobs,
and four other lovers before it lifted. Later,
he thanked me for being so cool. One man
I left handcuffed to a bed, since he was always nicer
unsatisfied. Once I tried an orgy but found myself
thinking in the middle of it all, this: *we're a pack*
of lions clawing, eating, roaring over the body
of a crippled zebra, which is also us. Then I fell in love
with the least pushy of the bunch and acted as if
he alone meant anything. We fell off the bed
to be alone. I saw him again only twice more,
since it required an eight-hour drive and I was poor. After
the second time, he decided he had to write a poem
right then and I put my clothes back on and sat
on his screened-in porch. Crickets, katydids, big
furry brown moths came to cling on the screens.

I examined their armored, hairy undersides with
cocktail toothpicks while his typewriter clattered.
What was the meaning of such machinery?
Cats howled and screamed. The poem went on for hours,
it seemed, and turned out only to be a letter
to his mother, who he said was crazy. I apologized
and took the next bus home. The next week
I was paying for a therapist, looking for
a personal trainer I wouldn't fall in love with.
That was a mistake too, since it meant I had only
myself to impress and that trick never works.
Once I slept with a man right after his wife died.
He said it was her last wish. Once a man promised
to make me a star. Once a man drove his brand new car
directly toward a tree to see if I'd flinch or scream,
which is how he recognized care. I said
I'd welcome death and groped his crotch. He
turned away. I had late night dates with another man
who turned out to look exactly like my father
when he was twenty five— in a photo I never saw—
thank God—until years later. I'd meet him
in his shower at precisely ten o'clock.
For a while I pretended to be the plumber
who needed to check out his pipes. After
that wore off, we'd usually end up sitting together
on the shower floor while hot water rained down. We'd
sit there and admire our feet getting cleaner
and cleaner near the drain. Usually he'd be drunk
before I even got there, and want to talk about
his first lover's suicide. When I wouldn't agree
to tie him up and then punch him until he fell asleep,
well, that was that. He yelled faggot at me
from a car once when I was walking on the street.
Once I slept with a man who was kind but
not attractive at all, just to see if I could make
what I thought was the right choice. Forget
running with scissors or dropping pennies off

the Empire State Building or swimming right after lunch.
There was only had to have, have, had, had it with.
One man I nearly killed myself over I ended up
laughing about. Another I laughed at then now I miss
like the best goddamned dog I ever knew, who
I could tell anything to, who listened even though
he could never help me which did help in the end.
I was ordering drinks on a plane to Europe
when he got put down. Sometimes I still
feel his big warm weight beside me in the night
and turn toward it before I think, oh, right.

Queer: some instructions

Queers play hopscotch. Queers shine at anything involving jumping one-legged in and out of boxes. Queers keep things up their blue sleeves: rabbits, muscles, French cologne. Queers go overboard every time something new happens to enter. Vinegar potato chips. Buttery suede pants. Queers throw themselves into things. And it is true that they are frequently thrown.

Queer choirs queer music. A penny falls from a bad pocket, from a too-late hand, a shine down the leg, a tinkle. Queer goes down as far as possible and rolls away. Oh, Queer of gutter, Queer of the perverse Paris where the hunchbank hunches, where the phantom destroys the great chandelier before time does. Queer goes crying down on its audience, a thousand bits of quartz, glass, reflection. Queers have no reflection. Nor can they abide sandwiches.

Queer in the treetops turning white. Queer in the little rapids melting stone. If a queer is beaten to death is he all alone? Do we count the one who does it? Even with his alibi of panic? Even with his terror of being touched? Queer on the rock where the bicyclists turn on their nearly invisible trails among the trees. The body itself another stump. The body itself a kind of Scandinavian furniture we beat together because of the unreadable instructions.

Queer at home in the sexual. Who will answer in the absence of a parent who worries too much about safety to the detriment of listening. Who else treats the sea like a sister? Who else rips off the shirt it took several hours to buy? Queer at home watching TV too. The thing is queer won't forget, even in the wee hours of the last breath, that it all was something. Queer's mistake is not regret. Even the boredom was awake.

In the Western Mountains

When I woke from a dream of losing my love,
(or was it my father again?) I woke up in tears.
Was there something about Istanbul? Across
the country this morning love was coming home
from nearly two weeks of business elsewhere.
He hadn't once called me. Meanwhile I was
going on nature walks, learning about Lodgepole pines,
whose survival strategies depend on the seeds,
the tree willing to burst into flame if that would make
its armored pinecones' seedvaults unlock. I touched
Jeffrey Pines with their 4 inch bark, their torqued trunk,
their thousand year lives, a strategy based on self. I had both
in mind—the martyrs who blew themselves up hoping
for heaven versus those long sufferers who stand up
their whole lives for justice. It was still dark outside,
whereas where he was would be light. He had not
called once. Meanwhile, outside my window a bird
I couldn't see to name began what we call singing,
pee-you, pee-you, pee-you, pee-you. When it finally stopped
I tried to send my thinking back to who
had been lost in the dream. What was left
was only grief, as clear a stream of it as yesterday
I'd walked my bare feet into, shirtless,
the fattening white loaf of my body
growing pink, turning gold. And it seemed
suddenly possible I made what's an old
mistake for me again: There was a fire
in the dream, but it might be I'd misjudged
excitement for grief. Meanwhile, David
was writing poems about his youngest son.
Meanwhile, Lisa called home everyday to talk.
Meanwhile, Emily rescued an old verb from silence.

When I opened the shower curtain and stepped in,
a small white moth flew up, banged against my knee,
my arm, knocked against my chest. I threw back

the curtain so it would see the light bulb on the ceiling
and go after it, but it continued to crash against me,
flapped against my throat, slapped against my ear
as if I were a raw filament, a bleached sheet
under a full moon, a bar of Dove, Lot's wife
changed and left to burn alone. Desperate,
I turned on the shower and stood in the first cold water,
just to get away from its wild terror.

Sapphics

1
Someone said "the sea" and I felt the ocean.
Someone said "it's over" and took my stutter.
Buildings darkened. Happiness barked a ways off.
After that, silence.

2
Not a lover trapped in the past forever;
Look toward, straight ahead, as a fortune said once.
Something's waiting breathlessly near the doorway.
Elephant patience.

3
Found three apples suddenly where only
Onions had been earlier, tearful, rustling.
Three red apples where there was nothing ready,
Edible. Ate them.

Salt

1

I have been craving that salary, that taste of the sea, that process by which the wild dead are cured toward eternity. Their huge shapes are already hanging in the basement, upside-down, near the furnace, in the dark like enormous bats. The sun goes down so early. The house fills up with warm. What's a little mineral then sprinkled on this and that? The sun goes off and this pure bite in every thing I eat? And then the water, water, water in me will not freeze while I fall asleep, which is all I do when the sunlight leaves.

2

Meanwhile, the individual kiss sticks to the lips an uncomfortable second. In another country, my bedroom would sleep six comfortably. It's hard to know when not to look. It's Lot's wife we remember, for her humanity at the last moment, like Orpheus who turned at the wrong moment, but for a reason we understand. It's hard not to turn into a strange pillar or smell the tang of the sea surging suddenly in the lover's neck. It's easy on the other hand to forget that Lot's story is this: afterward his daughters raped him, thinking there was no one else but them. They might better have stayed home.

3

You can see I've been mad about some things for a long time. It goes back to the old days of wind and sand, when fresh water was more valuable than gold. Before we discovered this other side of the world, where we could drink at last, where food and space is plentiful. Before we bought, by sweat and the use of the right words, this house with its enormous rooms. What are we always waiting for, we asked ourselves. And then I found you hadn't been waiting at all. And then you left, changed. And here I am turning and turning in the middle of the night, trying to remember what I'd eaten that might account for the taste of blood. And then taking the dog out to pee. And then looking up into the dash of stars.

4

What's left when the ocean recedes. What no joy should lack now, says Frost. I've learned at last to make soup more or less from scraps. A carcass for broth. Fingerling roots, the skins intact. Rosemary which grows gigantic on the back patio. Who will I call when I'm sad soon? For fluid balancing. For electrical signaling in the nervous system. For holy water. To exorcise, purify, kill the slugs who continue to rise out of nowhere and glide slimily over the strawberries. To burn them in their skins, for next day hornets to transform. I pick up the knife, the cord, the candle, the book. I sing a little song in the room in the dark.

Little Night Song

Sometimes I wake up thinking it's
someone trying the lock on the front door
in the middle of the night but
it's only the dog muttering something, rattling
his jaws at the end of the bed. Sometimes I
think it's rain but it's only the black dog
I rescued to keep me from thinking
certain kinds of thoughts. Often
I have to listen a long time until
I make out what it is that's there
in the room with me, a hot
fear that rises up immediately
and out of an old reason I still call
my father. Because he set my nerves
so early on to terror, to hide.
But listen, honestly, he's dead now,
and I'm old enough to take him on,
so how long can I continue to name
everything after him, call him the cause
of everything gone bad? Every day
the news brings stories of abuse
that make my childhood seem lucky.
And if I have this dog who occasionally
sounds like creaky stairs,
a jiggled knob, a kind of rain hitting
the window like small gravel, it is only
a memory of threat. If I were so concerned
that my father's here, I could
just walk downstairs to find him
smoking and drinking his coffee black,
sit down at the table in that darkness
and relax. He liked the quiet;
he drank it in. Maybe it's who else
might be at my table now that worries me.

Ink, Dank, Slender
for my brother

What is the trick to the dance of the ember:
its stink, its hard spank? In November
what I'll bring to Thanksgiving will never
compare to the pink baked hams my grandmother
would clink down amongst us on a platter,
the incarnation of manners.
The next afternoon my older brother
would be off again, kissing quick, back
to New York City bars and lovers
no one knew of. I think. There's a brand
of sweater he used to bring back that made
us wonder. I'd wait for the clank
of the shower curtain rings to walk
into his room. The spark of water. To sniff
for hints, wonder at the trick
of his apparent escape. He wore a pin,
a dark uniform, that summer he sent
thin postcards back from Algeria, Morocco,
the straits of Gibraltor. We didn't unpack
what we didn't want to matter. Last month,
at fifty, with rings, in Canada,
he married Ted, a lawyer. *In pink?* I ask,
or wearing the color of lilies, of lynx,
of banks of snow? Were there showers
of things? Confetti? Rice? *It was simple,*
he answered, which ends it. Let me
think in the dark of its splendor,
I said anyway. I couldn't remember
how to bear love, to be frank, without
being a monster, the id-thing, the rank
and filed claws of disaster. (I drink it.
I drank. I get hammered.
Water the next morning stinks.)
My heart's broken, I sing to my brother.
So was mine before this, he laughs.
There's always another. But
first you think salt, stone, over.

3

Midlife

In the balding, November woods,
the cardinal's blood freckle,
the dark phlegm of the crow,
the woodpecker pounding
his skull against a wall.

The Mouse

A heart as small as. An eye as black and alive. An impossible leafprint of a foot. Large sensitive ears, just as. Against the house settling or the furnace kicking on or the refrigerator's ice supply refilling or the knock of the washing machine's water. Those feet made of rice grain, of the chaff of rice, as small. For months, there was this stir at the corner of my eyes. I'd turn and it would be nothing. Maybe the guy next door died or something, I thought, a ghost. As if a pigeon flew between the sunlight and the back window again. I blinked the startle away. Then one day I opened the drawer full of silverware. The pills of its waste like lint. The midden I'd become. I held my breath and my heart began to pound. Down among the pipes and centipedes. Nights, at the light click, it runs right into a crack and through. As a thief if the space is safe enough. In the dim light of the middle of my life. As I am making decisions about what to do.

Poem for the Soles of my Feet

Constantly in the dark, wrapped
in cloth and tied down, blindfolded,
like loaves of bread, like fresh fish,
like hostages, walked all day into
dead ends, through loud traffic, through
crowds, silences, water, gravel, hallways
full of hot cardamom, fennel, secret
cigarettes, muffled laughter, until they
are too tired to remember how to send
blood back up the columns of the legs, bring
blood down upon themselves, sweating
into their masks, stuffed into tiny cars, faces
pressed into the heat of engines, the punch
of brakes, the slamming of doors, the pop
and shriek of locks, sudden pirouettes of
happiness, how they shuffle beneath us, growing
quietly, steadily desperate for the inexplicable
tickles and kisses of love, the slipping free
of covers to find another pair like themselves,
blazing like coals in the three a.m. darkness
and silence, and touching them with a tenderness
that surprises even themselves, that they still
have it in them, after all this time, like the fish
that wakes up in the pan and in its last second
forgives its devourer everything that will come next.

For the Small Hairs of My Nose

Given the chance I would go around apologizing for everything I
        do.
Given half a chance.
Given even an opening.

As if there were a sniper trained on me while I drive to work.
As if a serial killer were following me and listening
for evidence I beat my dog.

As if everything depended on my tiniest attention, my
not failing to register a shift in the wind,

Morning's thumb and forefinger pick me up out of bed
where I would otherwise lie in my various crusts.

Light flickers around me, a flock of pigeons
the neighbor empties out bags of bread for.
They startle, a plume of iridescent dust at the slightest sound.
They circle the houses then come back down
to her tiny concrete patio full of plastic flowers.

It helps clean the air, she told me once.

Lines for the Left Hand

Doing what, the right hand
doesn't always seem to know.
Having given up the work
of subtle textures, the snug
handshake, the little ways
dominance betrays its teeth,
it accepts the ring we
slip on it for its commitment,
to stay quiet, maintain balance,
flutter in occasional silliness.
It remembers a name before
your name; every so often
you need to see again what a wreck
it was before the right took over.
Life watches the margins for crumbs
it might pinch. It loves the napkin
where you unconsciously dabbed
away water or a too thick color
from your delicate brush
while you were trying to get right
flowers and made thistles.

For the Small Hairs on My Ears

If I am turning wolf-like, a wolflight
growing up within me now, how
past fifty feels, fur just waiting
to bristle, thistle, thorns, an urge
to sleep at noon, pace the house all night,
staring out through glass at strangers
coming back from nearby bars—

If I'm becoming something else,
listening at the crack in a wall for what
needs to be saved from itself, what
wants a surprise it can't speak,
hungry for the moon in whose silences
moths and spiders spin and moult,
something that might suddenly shift---

Horror on the tongue, a muzzle-
lick of light or fire, if there's hell,
if there's heaven, what's the use
of either eternity? I pick at whiskers
without much thought,
pinch the wiriest out, a sting, a
growl in the cafe as I listen to
the theological students whisper
together about what they want,
when it will be given them: the strength
to break the backs of monsters.

The Nests in Winter

Of course the point is to be hidden.
To seem like nothing, to be forgettable,
be passed by. Lonely little things now,
the size of my fist and with a lid of snow.
The trees whittled down to nothing.
It surprises me there were so many,
woven sticks, shuttled stalks of weed and grass,
the occasional scrap of blue or clear plastic,
proof of birds working invisibly in the world.
Right beside us. Even now. Even though
we can see right into the earliest light
in the universe. Even now that we can
count the atoms in a needle's eye.
I assume the nest builders will
be back. I assume they're not
following me around like a shadow
and will not sing. But I'm willing to
believe anything: that year after year
there arise secret nurseries right in front of us
in the small branches of the apricot trees,
themselves grown from pits
strangers on the river trail spat out.

Emptying the Octopus

Good luck to the one who finds the dream
of a blue cave strewn with big dumb shellfish.
Good luck to the one who finds the propellers,
the one tentacle inscribed with prophetic runes.
Good luck to the one who finds the decoder ring
for which gestures mean love, run, don't even--
Say the man behind you whispers *Get out at the next stop*
or tries to slip his hands through the cushions.
Good luck to the one who finds that old pearl hatpin
my grandmother used to hold up when we'd ask.
Good luck to the one who finds the fountain of ink,
the maps of the oceans, Christ's fraternity pin.
Good luck to the one who doesn't see the strange beak
always snapping at the bottom of the bed.
If he wants to be all hands, Grandma smiled. *Fine.*

The Equipage

That there are bees in my azaleas
despite the news of hives collapsing.

Begin again: branches of hot pink feathers,
fistfuls of fluted champagne, each
a barndoor open for the horses' return;
inside: the smell of oats, of sugar waiting.

Let winter be over, the careful tethering
of hope. No room for tears among these shriners
and their tiny circling vehicles. The bees
are in the dresses of the desperate debutants,
hearing bells, imagining candles lit for
Easter, each orange shrine a miracle.

Meanwhile, a tiny map of Pittsburgh etching itself
inside them, a dance to return with.

Among the white and green pantaloons
of the blueberry bushes, a nudge will open,
a tongue will flash forward. So the oranges grow,
the peachfuzz depends on, the cherries sing about
before they harden. So during a time of war,
the heart finds a strange mercy still,

a tiny hat, a gold coat full of messages.

Sunglassed, humming, their mouths complicated
with pins, forks, kazoos, full of implements,
these hungry priestesses imitate the bear
that would eat them, that shakes them off,
that steals their drunk. They rise to plumb
the morning glories, to answer riddle with koan;

like tiny cattle, they beat the fleshy silks into batter.
They fall upon them like rain, their transistors
turned up full for the carrying on, away.

Begin again: bring wheelbarrows for the hell of it.
It rubs off. Bring the horses to harness,
unwrap the footmen—

That March

The bird outside that morning was too insistent on territory,
one cheap note over and over.

Inside, still in bed, we touched each other's bodies so lightly
it felt like breathing.

This is mine, the bird kept saying. There you were,
writing on my back and shoulder, and

over your ribs, my
fingertips singing.

4

Having Read Tranströmer All Night

Woke up inside a keyhole. Coughed a nest of mice out of my throat.
Asked the dog if he'd been driving the bed last night
because it looked like we'd crashed into something.
He shook his skin. It was the sound of keys.

Begin, Again

In the beginning was a cough from the audience. God forgot his
lines. In the beginning was the chair squeak, the candy slowly
being unwrapped from its transparent cover, and God couldn't help
turning to look; thus the stumble came to life, rising quickly and
rushing up the aisle and through the double doors. Thumping.
In the beginning was the whisper, the cellphone vibrating like a
tiny cow in a black clutch near the ankles in the tenth row. God
grabbed an apple from the prop table just in time to cover
his nakedness.

Shift

Forgiveness is different, I tell her,
from amnesia. It doesn't mean I've let go
what happened, but I also can't remember
only broken hands and midnight fear. I know

he was a cruel man often, but what about
the summer he taught me to drive his red,
indestructible Ford truck at the sandpit?
Out in its canyons, on its hard-packed roads,

over bulldozer tracks, I grinded his gears,
around his great yellow cranes, forgot which was clutch,
which was brake, swerved on two wheels near
mud holes I had seen swallow vehicles much

larger than ours. Then, he had been my patient father,
saying brake, brake, brake, brake, brake.

Talking About the Curtains

Whatever it is we say
is never enough to hide
the way we feel. What
ever we do there
will always be something
blocking the truth. We
know this; we're stuck
with each other and
an imperfect blue, a
texture, a weight
and length we can't
return. What are we
doing, you filling your
time with food
instead of feelings, me
running out of words?
You can tell the matter
matters the way we can
go on about nothing.
It's fine, you say,
a line I know now
means you're not
at all happy. I sigh
and try to say
what I meant to mean,
which is stay
but there are conditions.

Saint Wrench

1

The more you see a thing the less you see it, the more it quiets into a minor character, an unnamed member of the Greek chorus as it turns and counter-turns while you soliloquize in the bathroom over the broken toilet seat about your own helplessness. Your own face alights on itself as the bowl refills, sighs, stops quivering. Here is the moment a hero is made, you think.

2

It is possible to imagine that the name Christ written in the sand by the first nervous devotees was not a fish but a wrench, a single form drop-forged, capable of removing bent nails from good wood, of turning suddenly the water back on after days of drought and renovation.

3

In the wrench's slippery eye the universe revolves around the earth. It doesn't recognize Galileo's cosmology as weight-bearing. A wrench dreams of holding and being held, of being the instrument by which things are made to turn, until everything is adjusted. It doesn't sing. It makes a minor silver clink. Opened, it's Hathor, the old moon goddess, her glittering horns.

4

Each face is made up of a pair of minor faces, one that angles up, one that looks down its nose. Forced together they grow hungry for something to talk about. They will latch onto anything. Your fingernails, for instance. Your teeth. Anything to make you start.

The Dream of The Grandfathers

In one part we were birds. In another grandkids.
We were sure we were going to be locked away again.
At one point, there were beagles we tried to pick up
and run away with. Then they changed too.
The trick, I know, is to turn around and face
the thing that seems terrible and look it in the eyes.
If it has eyes. In which case, look in the place
a face wants to be. In that case, your grandfather
might appear, who will let you swing from his hands
while you scream *Wheee,* having almost forgotten
(or had you not known?) how much you needed
his old troll-like strength, to be tossed around
with the other kids or birds or leaves you were
when it was done and the walls returned
to the walls and the floor once more became
the sound of your breathing in the dark again.

Dream of the Wild Pig

1
He was supposed to be dead, my father,
not at the old farm house, that big brick one
our family built before the Revolution.
Around it, enormous lawns rustled with neglect.
His breathing was hard, old, enormous.
I knew I should have grabbed the mowers myself
and simply done the mowing like a good son.
Like any simply practical person would have.
But I just wanted him to go to sleep again.

2
When we drove by later, in a huge Oldsmobile,
I ducked down seeing him out, frail, still coughing,
fidgeting around where the lawn met the road. The big
riding mower purred behind him as he put clippings in
a large plastic bag. Even on his deathbed, I thought,
he can't leave well enough alone. The large older woman
who was driving me somewhere looked down at me.
I'll explain later, I said.

3
But of course I never did. We were sitting outside at
what was half-picnic, half-farmer's market, half-town meeting.
Everyone was eating and either gossiping or listening.
I turned to the woman on my left to tell her, yes,
I was living here now, back from the big cities of the world,
when I saw over her shoulder a boar with the horns of a steer
running toward us. She stood up but it knocked her down.
Other women ran over to help her, leaving no one else
to stop the danger. I grabbed some leftover rope
thin as curtain pulls and threw them over the pig's head.
Its horns were gone by now, and with the rope on,
the thing relaxed enough I could wrestle it down.
And there was a kind of meanness in me I recognized,
and suddenly we were at a barbeque, and on the spit,

the pig was pissing all over itself with fear,
turning gold then bronze. Still alive, upside-down.
I wasn't afraid to kill it, I don't think.
It wasn't that. It was how best to do it.
The crowd gathered around. I had a knife. And here
came the man who'd show me how to use it.

Icarus

I suppose someday somewhere someone will
write about what might have been if only
I'd listened and flown straight the way he thought
I would. How we'd arrive out of sunlight,

from a blue sky, first specks then birds then large
enough to alert some king who'd send out
a party. How we'd be welcomed of course
and maybe there'd be a moment of relief,

but after hearing our story soon enough
anyone with something to protect would
turn us back to making weapons and prisons.
Would that have been better than what happened?

If I'd been obedient? It's a father's
story you've heard all these years, made itself
out of wax and gulls and myths about the sun.
The wings alone wouldn't have liberated anyone.

Dream of the Lawns

Yet another yelling match with my father, in which
this time he'd taken out a whole tall hedge that bordered
my house and the neighbors' without asking me,
assuming wherever he was was his house, his
to do as he wanted. Took out a beautiful green wall
that gave shade, that housed birds, that made
privacy possible. Then sat down. He wasn't even drinking
when I found him talking to an old student of mine.
First I was stunned and said, oh buddy, what did you do,
what did you do over and over until he grew
irritated. It's my house, he said, I'll do what I want.
Just like he always did. And at first I was willing to
let it go, deal with it, shrug it off, drink the lemonade
of summer. Because it was summer and the lawns exposed
were a beautiful green together, as my father
was a young man again, even a handsome actor
with strong muscles, bronze tan. He was the last man
in our family who could have done such work
himself, by hand, and it's true I resent him for that.
I got up the courage and confronted him later
under a tree in the back yard, saying he was wrong,
it was my house, my name was on the lease,
I paid for the place (though here I also knew
part of my money was because of his--a lie I thought
even in the dream was true, sadly). I got right in his face
with this, which was as close in the dream as I got
to saying Remember what you did to us night
after night, coming home drunk, irresponsible,
threatening, a constant danger, until I had back
my old anger which turned him into a man again
and not a symbol. I woke up from all my shouting
as I used to when he came home after 2 am
and my mother'd meet him in the living room
with her own litany of disappointments. Only this time
there was nothing real to fear, only the mockingbird
claiming the whole world was his on the neighbor's roof.

Still, I have begun putting up a two by four against
the front door at night. I don't want him back
that way anymore, although I do need someone
to help me fix the stair broken last summer by mistake.
How much I miss being the little boy
whose father with his bare hands could repair
anything that broke. I'm still the child who listens
to birds before morning, who prefers to watch things
move around him, who'd turn invisible if possible, be
secretary to the thousand things, the billion forms.
I was the one who sat on the porch with my mother
during thunder storms and counted seconds to see
how far away the lightning was. I watched things happen
and wrote about it. Then saw again and got angry.
Always words first then feelings after.
I know he was thinking he'd made my life better
in the dream; he'd simplified things; but that was his way
and not mine. I like to sit in the shadow of time's
overgrown hedge, always protected on one side.
I like to watch what appears when no one moves.

Wax and Wings

I am sorry that sometimes I seem to only respond to love with
    silence.

I have often been unable to control when my tongue stops.

I am sorry that I often sing when I'm alone.

The night and my snoring go without saying.

I am sorry some mornings to wake and turn to you to find you gone,
    in the other room, sleeping.

Thank god you bought that coffeemaker. I couldn't remember every
    morning the ratio of spoons to cups.

You need your coffee the way I need to walk the dog every morning.

I am sorry to keep bringing up the landfills full of K-cups piling up
    around us.

There are some things that can be mended but not while you're
    wearing them.

I was clear ahead of time I'd be paying for the dinner and we both
    had a wonderful time imagining a future elsewhere.

I went with the Courvoisier and you had a French Manhattan. They
    were both delicious and too much.

It was too much fun to keep laughing. I'm always sorry when it ends.

It is a problem I know to keep asking you to remind me of things.

I am sorry to have brought up my old love who dyes his hair after
    you brought up your old fling who had had a wart removed.

You were texting your sister when I was overhearing the next table's
    conversation.

There is your inability to admit you might be wrong about
    something as much as mine.

There we were, as happy as people who hadn't rolled up their change the day before.

I had the pot en feu and you had the salmon.

I'm sorry to have only imagined the roof leaking when you said you were hoping for a big snow.

And when you brought up moving away, I could only talk about the dog's discomfort.

I am sorry thinking the wings will not be enough for two.

I love when you put your arms out and I disappear into them.

I am sorry for thinking very often you are not careful enough; it is so easy to make a fatal mistake.

There will always be the problem of feeling held back, I'm afraid.

We had such a good time imagining we will learn French and move far away.

I am sorry that I often say a hard thing thinking it's a true thing and thinking you need to wake up.

I hate waking up to find you elsewhere and my mouth hollowed out and dry.

Honey

I don't buy it so much to use as to display it in the kitchen, near the tea kettle, where it warms the corner like a miniature sun or a rhyming dictionary. In the middle of the night, I sometimes sneak downstairs, unscrew the cap, slip a spoon out of the drawer, and put a spoonful of that impossible product of a hundred lives, a thousand flowers, a million pounds of light and heat and rainfall quietly into my mouth.

The Song

No one knows anyone who knows the song Orpheus
invented in Hades anymore. But it must have had
delight in it. Think about what it was up against,
what it's like to sing in the tomb, wanting love. Yes,
to burnt Eggplant Parmesan. Yes, to warm weight
of love in the middle of the night snoring and you
have to choose between pushing him out of bed
or learning to live with it for everything else you'd miss.
Against the queen of the dead's boredoms, her schedules
among the various houses of heroes and suicides
and drunks and martyrs she had only to nod to. To
break that heart enough she would turn to her god who
was more odor than man, whose fingers were roots,
whose eyes glittered but never ached except that once
long ago when he saw her. The gravesite for the singer
widens. It's possible to make out of air and fingers and
years of paying attention some space for the impossible.
Whether it's possible to bring back the same is
the problem. Orpheus couldn't. The wife of Lot.
Neither of them idiots or charlatans or hardhearted.
Just the reverse. They knew how to give, where to love,
how to thank the gods in the room, knew who else
was listening. And yet in an instant of doubt all of it
taken away. I've spent most of my life thinking about that.
My black lab has mastered the art of coming up the stairs
at night without making a sound. Sometimes
he follows me up when I go to sleep and jumps onto
the big bed with me. Sometimes he waits until
I have settled and turned the light off before he arrives
and throws his heavier darkness onto my feet. It's
a little like living with a demon, a thought you can't,
now that you've thought it, let go of. You have to
see it to its end, however painful, whatever sacrifices.
Even love suffers. You have to go forward and not look back
say the stories. There will be another lover. Surely.
Mathematics says there must be hundreds who might do.

Astronomy and physics imply millions just waiting, new
houses, landscapes, job prospects, dimensions. But,
the song says, recycling history, But. It doesn't want to solve
for X. It dissolves in Y. It makes a stutter in the step
of the choruses whose promises seem too easy to make.
It makes each body feel the weight of its want, even
the queen of the dead who'd long given up knowing
what she was married to for the comforts it afforded.
Suddenly she remembered and couldn't stand it
and told Orpheus yes, take her, anything to get rid of you,
but beware not to look too hard at what you're asking for.
I think you know what I'm saying. Your song does.
Have you listened to it yourself? The cold feet in the night.
The arguments about garbage and toothpaste and family.
Most of love isn't singing but schedules and nodding. Most of it
is forgetting and not knowing. Yes, some of it is piercing
and being pierced. Some of that is worth keeping. Some
of that. Think of how much easier it is to live alone
with a good dog who obeys you and guards the house
while you're sleeping. Why isn't that enough? Why not
simply be happy you had it once? Somewhere in the story,
maybe the story itself, I keep thinking, is an answer. Maybe
love's impossible to ask for and impossible to save,
and after we've admitted that, we still have to live.

Jeff Oaks is the author of four chapbooks, *The Unknown Country, The Moon of Books, Shift,* and *Mistakes with Strangers.* This is his first full-length collection. He has published poems in a number of literary magazines, including *Assaracus, Best New Poets, Field, Georgia Review, Missouri Review, Superstition Review,* and *Tupelo Quarterly.* A recipient of a Pittsburgh Foundation Grant and three Pennsylvania Council of the Arts fellowships, he teaches writing at the University of Pittsburgh.

CPSIA information can be obtained
at www.ICGtesting.com
Printed in the USA
LVHW081827160220
647098LV00012B/974